VELOCIRAPTOR

AND OTHER SMALL, SPEEDY MEAT-EATERS

Prehistoric World

VELOCIRAPTOR

AND OTHER SMALL, SPEEDY MEAT-EATERS

VIRGINIA
SCHOMP

BENCHMARK BOOKS

MARSHALL CAVENDISH
NEW YORK

DINOSAURS LIVED MILLIONS OF YEARS AGO. EVERYTHING WE KNOW ABOUT THEM—HOW THEY LOOKED, WALKED, ATE, FOUGHT, MATED, AND RAISED THEIR YOUNG—COMES FROM EDUCATED GUESSES BY THE SCIENTISTS WHO DISCOVER AND STUDY FOSSILS. THE INFORMATION IN THIS BOOK IS BASED ON WHAT MOST SCIENTISTS BELIEVE RIGHT NOW. TOMORROW OR NEXT WEEK OR NEXT YEAR, NEW DISCOVERIES COULD LEAD TO NEW IDEAS. SO KEEP YOUR EYES AND EARS OPEN FOR NEWS FLASHES FROM THE PREHISTORIC WORLD!

With thanks to Dr. Mark A. Norell, Chairman of the Division of Paleontology, American Museum of Natural History, for his expert review of the manuscript.

Benchmark Books
Marshall Cavendish
99 White Plains Road
Tarrytown, New York 10591-9001
www.marshallcavendish.com

©Marshall Cavendish Corporation 2003

Library of Congress Cataloging-in-Publication Data

Schomp, Virginia.
Velociraptor and other small, speedy meat-eaters / by Virginia Schomp.
    p. cm. - (Prehistoric world)
Includes index and bibliographical references.
Summary: Describes the physical characteristics and behavior of Velociraptor and other small, speedy meat-eating dinosaurs.
ISBN 0-7614-1025-2
    1. Velociraptor—Juvenile literature. 2. Carnivora, Fossil—Juvenile literature. 3. Dinosaurs—Juvenile literature.
    [1. Velociraptor. 2. Dinosaurs.] I. Title.
QE862.S3 S4 2002   567.912-dc21   2001043987

Front cover: *Velociraptor*   Back cover: *Oviraptor*   Pages 2–3: *Dromaeosaurus*

Photo Credits:

Cover illustration: Marshall Cavendish Corporation

The illustrations and photographs in this book are used by permission and through the courtesy of:
Corbis: Reuters NewMedia Inc., 25. *Marshall Cavendish Corporation:* 2-3, 11, 12, 13, 14, 17, 18, 19, 20-21, 22, 23, 24, back cover. *The Natural History Museum, London:* Orbis, 8. *Photo Researchers, Inc.:* Francois Gohier, 9.

Map and Dinosaur Family Tree by Robert Romagnoli

Printed in Hong Kong
1 3 5 6 4 2

For Christopher and Amanda

Contents

THE FIGHTING DINOSAURS

The horned dinosaur Protoceratops *had powerful jaws for defense against sharp-clawed* Velociraptor.

A small, hungry *Velociraptor* prowls the Mongolian desert. Its keen eyes spot fresh meat—a baby horned *Protoceratops*. Swiftly the hunter pounces . . . and comes face-to-face with the baby's mother. Lowering her head, the adult horned dinosaur charges. In the fierce battle, *Protoceratops* crushes *Velociraptor*'s chest, while the hunter slashes the mother's belly with its wicked claws. Weak and bleeding, the dinosaurs collapse. Soft sand covers their bodies. Eighty million years later, scientists will dig up the fossil bones of these ancient enemies, still locked in combat.

The "fighting dinosaurs" fossils helped paleontologists (scientists who study prehistoric life) learn how dinosaurs fought and defended themselves. The discovery also proved something the scientists already suspected—that little *Velociraptor* was one of the fiercest members of a group of dinosaurs known as theropods.

The life-and-death struggle of a Protoceratops *and* Velociraptor *has been preserved through the centuries in the famous "fighting dinosaurs" fossils.*

Theropods were two-legged predators—meat-eaters that hunted other animals for food. Many kinds of theropods lived at different times during the Age of Dinosaurs. Some were giants, like towering *Tyrannosaurus*. Others were small but deadly. The chart on page 26 shows how *Velociraptor* and the other small theropods fit into the dinosaur family tree.

The Age of Dinosaurs

Dinosaurs walked the earth during the Mesozoic era, also known as the Age of Dinosaurs. The Mesozoic era lasted from about 250 million to 65 million years ago. It is divided into three periods: the Triassic, Jurassic, and Cretaceous.

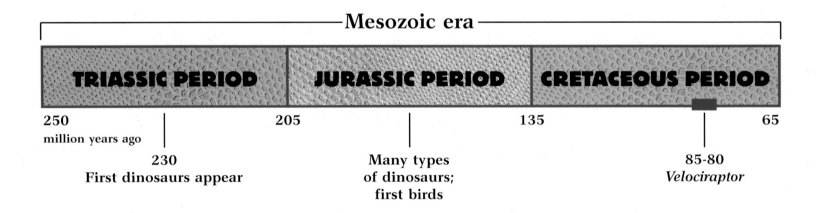

Mesozoic era

| TRIASSIC PERIOD | JURASSIC PERIOD | CRETACEOUS PERIOD |

250
million years ago

205

135

65

230
First dinosaurs appear

Many types
of dinosaurs;
first birds

85-80
Velociraptor

Utahraptor

Deinonychus

Velociraptor

Theropods came in many sizes—some smaller than Velociraptor*, some more than twice as big as twenty-foot* Utahraptor.

With its slender, hollow-boned body and long legs, Coelophysis was fast enough to capture speedy lizards and other small prey.

COELOPHYSIS
(see-loh-FIE-sis)
When: Late Triassic,
225–205 million years ago
Where: western United States
◆ **One of the earliest known dinosaurs**
◆ **Sometimes ate its own young**

TINY TERRORS

What they lacked in size, small theropods made up for in speed, smarts, and weapons. *Coelophysis,* one of the first theropods, may have chased its "fast food" at speeds up to twenty-five miles an hour. Wolf-sized *Troodon* was supersmart. With its big eyes and brain, this little predator was especially good at hunting smaller animals *and* avoiding larger hunters.

The prize for best weapon goes to *Velociraptor* and its cousins in the dromaeosaur family. Dromaeosaurs were small, ferocious theropods with one huge, curved claw on each foot. When they attacked, they could have snapped those claws forward like switchblades to slash at their unlucky victims.

COMPSOGNATHUS
(komp-sog-NAY-thus)
When: Late Jurassic,
150–135 million years ago
Where: Germany and France
◆ One of the smallest dinosaurs
◆ Skull 2 1/2 inches long

Chicken-sized Compsognathus *may have looked like a giant—but only to the insects and lizards it hunted for food.*

Many paleontologists believe that Troodon *was the most intelligent dinosaur (about as smart as a modern bird), because it had the biggest brain compared to its body size.*

RAPTOR FACTS

In the movie *Jurassic Park, Velociraptor* was taller than a person. In real life, it was only about the size of a large dog. But this fierce flesh-eater was still one of the most savage and dangerous killers of the dinosaur world.

Velociraptor had about eighty sharp, jagged teeth in its long, narrow snout. It ran fast on powerful legs, holding its tail straight out behind. Razor-sharp claws tipped its long fingers. Its toes also ended in claws—including the four-inch "switchblade" on each foot. Those killer claws sliced through flesh like a knife through butter. They were *Velociraptor*'s best weapon, both for snaring prey and fighting off predators.

HOT OR COLD?

One of the hottest arguments among paleontologists is whether dinosaurs were cold- or warm-blooded. Cold-blooded animals such as lizards and other reptiles cannot control their body temperature. They must lie in the sun to warm up and the shade to cool down. Warm-blooded animals, including birds and mammals, produce heat from the food they eat and have different ways of cooling down, such as panting or sweating.

Dinosaurs were reptiles. To some paleontologists, that means they were probably cold-blooded. Others argue that only warm-blooded animals could have been as quick and active as *Velociraptor* and its small, fierce relatives. A third group of scientists believe that dinosaurs were a bit of both—some warm-blooded, some cold-blooded, and some with ways of gaining and losing heat completely different from any modern animal.

A LOST WORLD

At the beginning of the Age of Dinosaurs, the earth had one huge super-continent, surrounded by a giant sea. This landmass eventually broke up, and the pieces drifted to form the continents we know today.

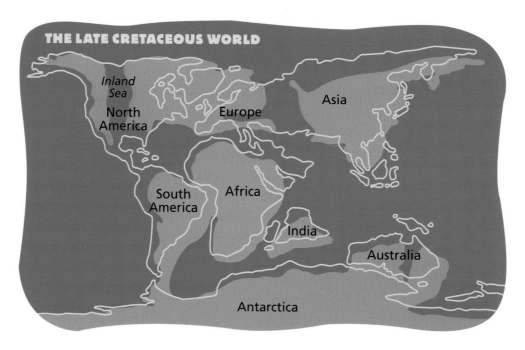

By the end of the Cretaceous period, the world was starting to look like it does today. The yellow outlines on the map show the shape of the modern continents; the green shading shows their position around eighty million years ago, in the days of Velociraptor.

Velociraptor lived toward the end of the Age of Dinosaurs, during the Late Cretaceous period. The world was warmer and wetter then. An inland sea stretched from the top to the bottom of North America, cutting the continent in half. For most of the Cretaceous period, the western half

DROMAEOSAURUS
(droh-mee-oh-SORE-us)
When: Late Cretaceous,
75–70 million years ago
Where: Alberta, Canada
♦ Forward-facing eyes for good
vision
♦ Ran fast on long legs

Like its cousin Velociraptor, Dromaeosaurus *kept the "switchblade" claws on its feet sharp by holding them off the ground when it walked.*

of North America was connected to Asia by a narrow land bridge. Small theropods lived on both sides of this bridge. Some even roamed back and forth, terrorizing tasty creatures on two continents.

DANGEROUS NEIGHBORHOODS

Let's take a tour of *Velociraptor*'s world. We must travel back in time eighty million years, to the Gobi Desert of central Asia. Today that region is a

Some Oviraptor *had odd-looking headgear, including small bumps and tall bony crests, which may have been brightly colored like the crests of some modern birds.*

OVIRAPTOR
(OH-vee-rap-tor)
When: Late Cretaceous,
80–68 million years ago
Where: Mongolia and China
- Short, toothless beak
- Some species had tall crests on their snouts

mostly dry, windswept wasteland. But in *Velociraptor*'s time, many different animals lived among the desert's scattered lakes and streams. We might see small lizards and scurrying mammals. Insects buzz overhead and burrow underground. Among the larger animals in the desert are two odd-looking plant-eaters: armored *Pinacosaurus* and horned *Protoceratops*.

These peaceful dinosaurs must keep a constant lookout for their nasty, meat-eating neighbors. Most of the small theropods, like tooth-less *Oviraptor,* dine on mammals, lizards, and insects. But the scariest of them all, *Velociraptor,* is a threat to much larger prey.

Velociraptor was a small, fast meat-eating dinosaur that may have traveled in fierce hunting packs.

PREDATORS AND PARENTS

What could be scarier than a hungry *Velociraptor* on the hunt? Two or three *Velociraptor!* Many paleontologists believe that some small theropods were smart enough to hunt in packs. By working together, these clever killers could attack much larger dinosaurs, the way a modern pack of wolves brings down a big reindeer or moose.

Two bloodthirsty Velociraptor *attack a less well-armed theropod, toothless* Oviraptor.

The leader of a *Velociraptor* pack scans the desert for fresh meat. It spots a relative—the small, toothless theropod *Oviraptor*. Dashing across the sand, the pack attacks its victim. One of the hunters grips the *Oviraptor*'s head with its clawed fingers. Another lashes out with its hooked toe claws. As the doomed dinosaur falls, the pack swarms over its body. Gouging out chunks of flesh with their sharp teeth, the *Velociraptor* feast.

Paleontologists have found Deinonychus *skeletons and teeth mixed in with fossils of a plant-eater more than twice its size—evidence that this brainy cousin of* Velociraptor *probably hunted in small, deadly packs.*

IN THE NEST

Menacing, murderous . . . and motherly? Scientists believe that some theropods were caring parents who took good care of their young.

A few years ago, fossil hunters in the Gobi Desert discovered the skeleton of a small theropod sitting on a nest of eggs. The toothless dinosaur, named *Citipati,* was a close relative of *Oviraptor.* It may have been keeping its eggs warm, the way modern birds do. Or it may have died trying to protect them from flowing sand during a fierce rainstorm.

Inside other theropod nests, scientists have found the remains of small plant-eaters. Perhaps a parent brought the freshly killed meat for its babies to eat. One *Citipati* nest held a special surprise: the crushed skulls of two young theropods related to the supersmart predator *Troodon.* Sometimes, it seems, even a fierce meat-eater could become just a snack for a hungry relative.

Oviraptor and other small theropods may have sat on their nests like big ground-dwelling birds, to hatch and protect their eggs.

DINOSAURS FOREVER

Throughout the Mesozoic era, hundreds of different kinds of dinosaurs appeared and became extinct—the last of their kind died out. Eighty million years ago, *Velociraptor* became extinct. Sixty-five million years ago—for reasons scientists still don't understand—the last of the dinosaurs disappeared. Or did they?

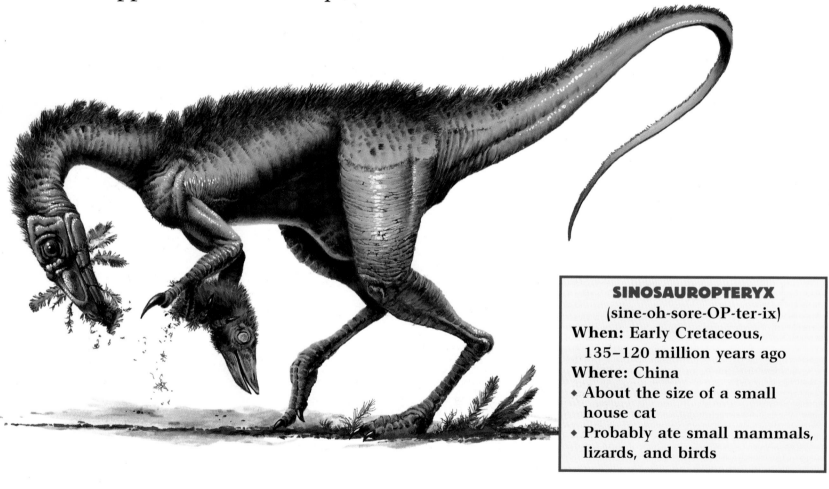

SINOSAUROPTERYX
(sine-oh-sore-OP-ter-ix)
When: Early Cretaceous,
  135–120 million years ago
Where: China
◆ About the size of a small
  house cat
◆ Probably ate small mammals,
  lizards, and birds

The tiny theropod Sinosauropteryx *was covered with hairlike feathers and may have dined on a distant relative, the early birds.*

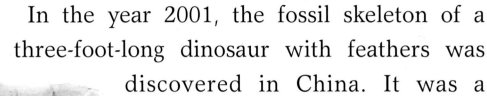

In the year 2001, the fossil skeleton of a three-foot-long dinosaur with feathers was discovered in China. It was a dromaeosaur—a small, fast-running cousin of *Velociraptor*. To many scientists, the discovery was proof that dinosaurs are related to modern birds. They believe that dinosaurs and birds are alike in so many ways—from their bones to their feathers to the way they cared for their young—that they must have come from the same distant ancestor. If that's true, says one paleontologist, "the dinosaurs did not disappear. They simply flew away."

This 130-million-year-old fossil skeleton proved that some small theropods had feathers—not for flying but probably for keeping warm—and may have been related to modern birds.

Dinosaur Family Tree

ORDER
All dinosaurs are divided into two large groups, based on the shape and position of their hipbones. Saurischians had forward-pointing hipbones.

SUBORDER
Theropods were two-legged meat-eating dinosaurs.

INFRAORDER
Tetanurans had stiffened (not flexible) tails. Ceratosaurs had hollow bones and four fingers.

FAMILY
A family includes one or more types of closely related dinosaurs.

GENUS
Every dinosaur has a two-word name. The first word tells us what genus, or type, of dinosaur it is. The genus plus the second part of a dinosaur's name tell us its species—the group of very similar animals it belongs to. (For example, *Velociraptor mongoliensis* is one species of *Velociraptor*.)

Scientists organize all living things into groups, according to features shared.
This chart shows the groupings of the small, fast meat-eaters in this book.

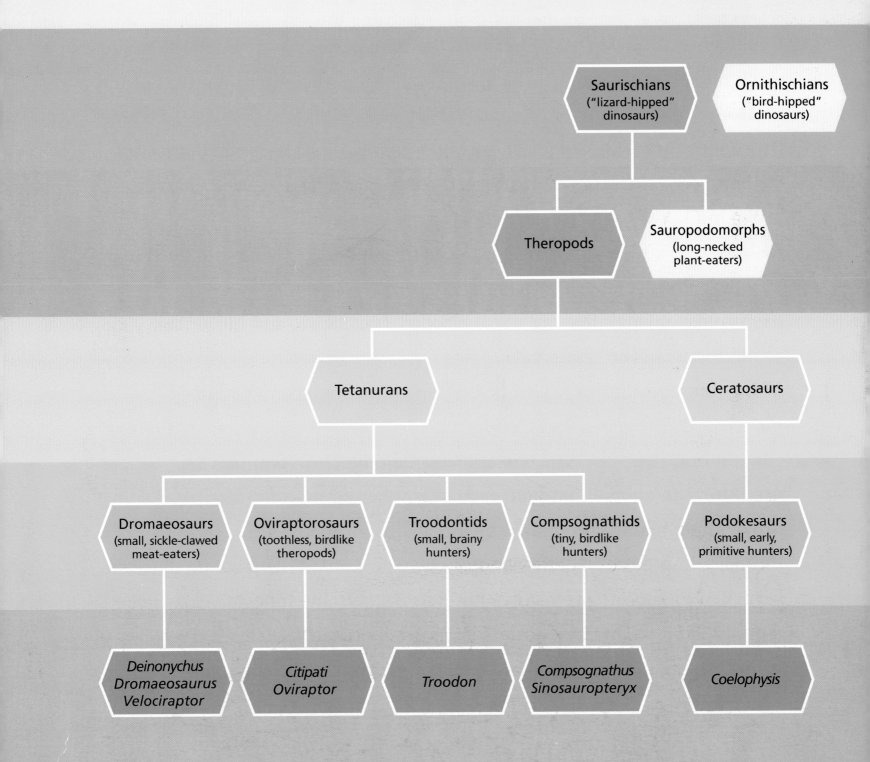

Glossary

Cretaceous (krih-TAY-shus) **period:** the time period from about 135 million to 65 million years ago, in which *Velociraptor* and the other members of the dromaeosaur family of theropods lived

dromaeosaurs (DROH-mee-oh-sores): a family of small to medium-sized theropods with large brains, jagged teeth, and a large curved claw on the second toe of each foot; sometimes called raptors

fossils: the hardened remains or traces of animals or plants that lived many thousands or millions of years ago

mammals: animals that are warm-blooded, breathe air, and nurse their young with milk; humans are mammals

Mongolia: a country in eastern Asia, between Russia and China

Pinacosaurus (pin-ack-oh-SORE-us): a small armored plant-eating dinosaur that lived in China and Mongolia at the same time as *Velociraptor*

predator: an animal that hunts and kills other animals for food

prey: an animal that is hunted by a predator for food

Protoceratops (proh-toh-SER-oh-tops): a small horned plant-eating dinosaur, related to *Triceratops*, that lived in Asia at the same time as *Velociraptor*

reptiles: animals that have scaly skin and, in most cases, lay eggs; crocodiles, turtles, and dinosaurs are reptiles, and many scientists also include birds in this group

Find Out More

BOOKS

Amery, Heather. *Looking at Velociraptor.* Milwaukee: Gareth Stevens, 1994.

Dingus, Lowell, and Mark A. Norell. *Searching for Velociraptor.* New York: HarperCollins, 1996.

Gillette, J. Lynett. *Dinosaur Ghosts: The Mystery of Coelophysis.* New York: Dial Books for Young Readers, 1997.

The Humongous Book of Dinosaurs. New York: Stewart, Tabori, and Chang, 1997.

Lessem, Don. *Raptors! The Nastiest Dinosaurs.* Boston: Little Brown, 1996.

Marshall, Chris, ed. *Dinosaurs of the World.* 11 vols. New York: Marshall Cavendish, 1999.

ON-LINE SOURCES *

Dino Russ's Lair: Dinosaur and Vertebrate Paleontology Information at
http://www.isgs.uiuc.edu/dinos/dinos_home.html

> Created by geologist Russ Jacobson, this website includes a very useful collection of links to museums and other organizations that provide on-line information about dinosaurs.

Lost World Studios at **http://www.lostworldstudios.com/exhibits/exhibits.html**

> Take a look at lifelike models of *Velociraptor* and its fierce cousins, created for museums and science centers.

Worldwide Museum of Natural History: Dinosaur Galleries at
http://www.wmnh.com/wmvd0000.htm

> The exhibits in this on-line museum of dinosaur fossils from the western United States include Bambi, a beautifully preserved baby *Velociraptor* found in Montana.

Zoom Dinosaurs at **http://www.zoomdinosaurs.com**

> This colorful, entertaining site from Enchanted Learning Software includes a world of information on dinosaur-related topics: dinosaur myths, records, behavior, and fossils; dinosaur fact sheets; quizzes, puzzles, printouts, and crafts; tips on writing a school report; and more.

*Website addresses sometimes change. For more on-line sources, check with the media specialist at your local library.

Index

Virginia Schomp grew up in a quiet suburban town in northeastern New Jersey, where eight-ton duck-billed dinosaurs once roamed. In first grade she discovered that she loved books and writing, and in sixth grade she was named "class bookworm," because she always had her nose in a book. Today she is a freelance author who has written more than thirty books for young readers on topics including careers, animals, ancient cultures, and modern history. Ms. Schomp lives in the Catskill Mountain region of New York with her husband, Richard, and their son, Chip.